CONTENTS

How To Use This Book

1. All you need is a pencil, eraser and paper. You can use anything you want to draw or paint with.

2. Start from step one and draw the black lines. Add the new black lines from steps two to four. The lines you have drawn already are shown in grey.

3. When you are ready, try drawing it by yourself.

4. Add your own colour to the finished drawing.

5. If you find it difficult, try tracing the steps or the final picture to practice and then try again.

6. Use lots of different drawings together on the same paper to make fun scenes and landscapes. What will you create?

7. Have fun!

I hope you enjoy this book!

I love hearing from readers and parents. Join my email newsletter by scanning the QR code below.

Scan the code to get free activity sheets, a free picture book and early reader copies of my new books for free:

Happy drawing!

Adrian Laurent

ISBN 978-0-473-59296-7 (paperback)

www.adrianlaurent.com

This Book Belongs To:

_____

Horse

①

②

③

④

Giraffe

①

②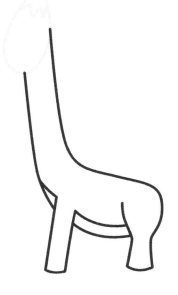

③

④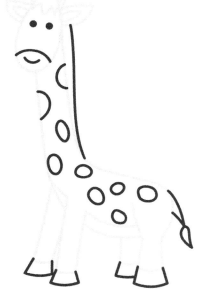

Cow

①

②

③

④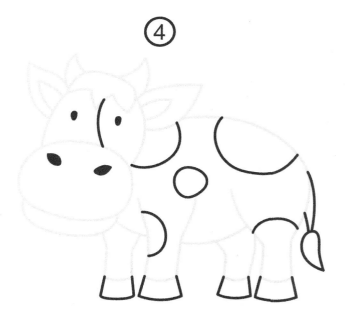

Sheep

①

②

③

④

Tiger

①

②

③

④

Duck

①

②

③

④

Alligator

① ②

③ ④

Lion

 ①

 ②

③

④

Llama

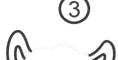

Fox

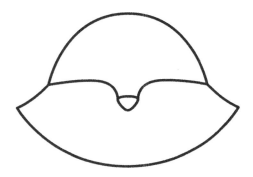

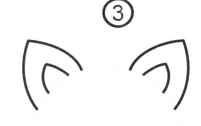

Bird

①

②

③

④

Bee

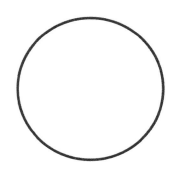

Snail

① ② ③ ④

Cat

①

②

③

④

Dog

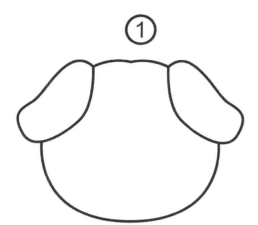
①

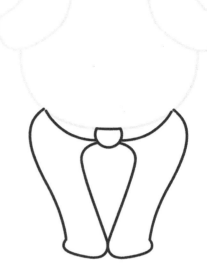
②

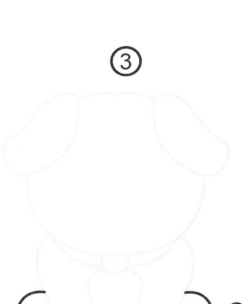
③

④

Narwhal

①

②

③

④

Lizard

①

②

③

④

Owl

Snake

①

②

③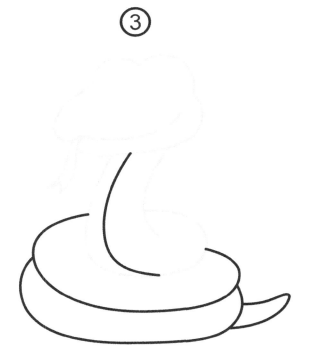

④

Fish

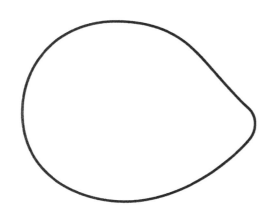

Elephant

①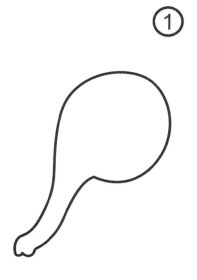

②

③

④

Butterfly

①

②

③

④

Dolphin

①

②

③

④

Beetle

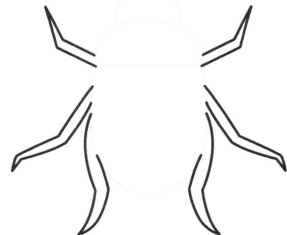

①

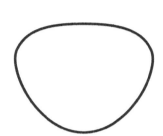

②

③

④

Octopus

①

②

③

④

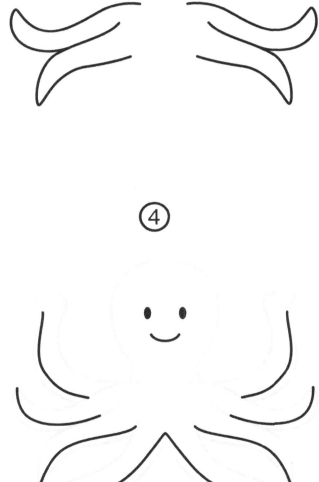

Chicken

①

②

③

④

Whale

① ② ③ ④

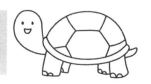

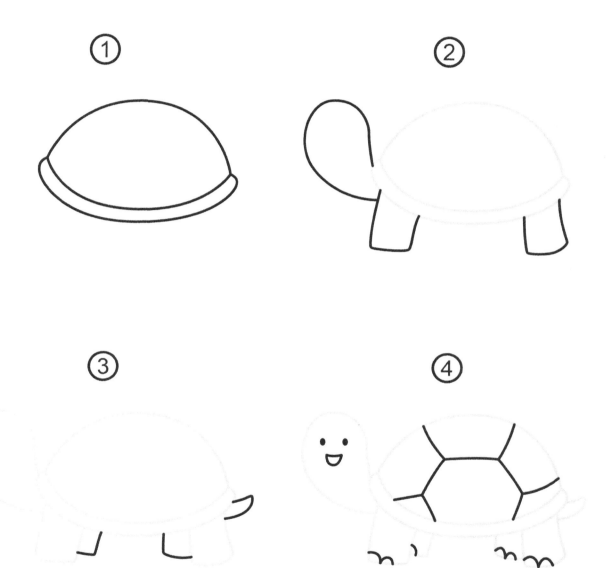

T-rex

① ②

③ ④

Triceratops

①

②

③

④

Pterodactyl

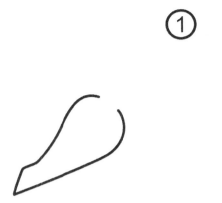

①

②

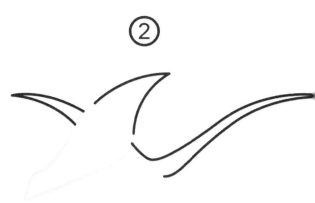

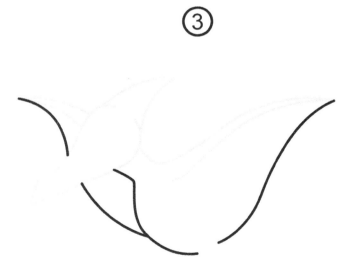

③

④

Unicorn

① ② ③ ④

Mermaid

①

②

③

④

Magic Wand

①

②

③

④

Castle

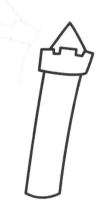

Princess

Fairy

①

②

③

④

Alien

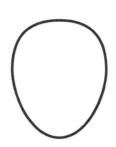

Car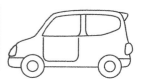

①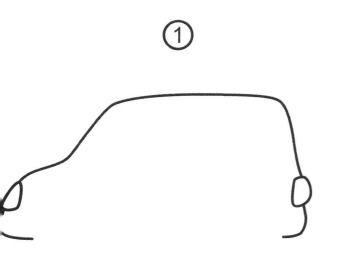

②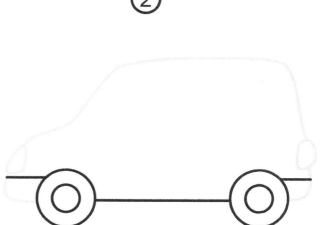

③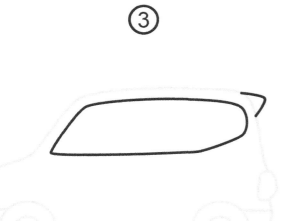

④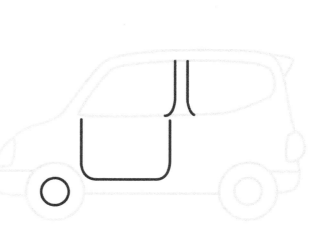

Truck

①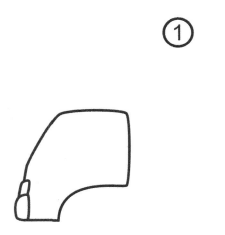

②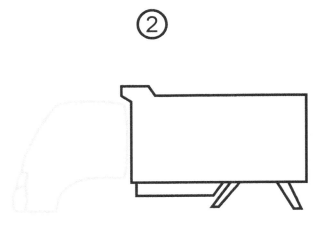

③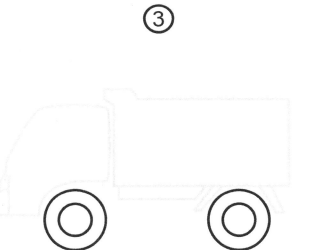

④

Monster Truck

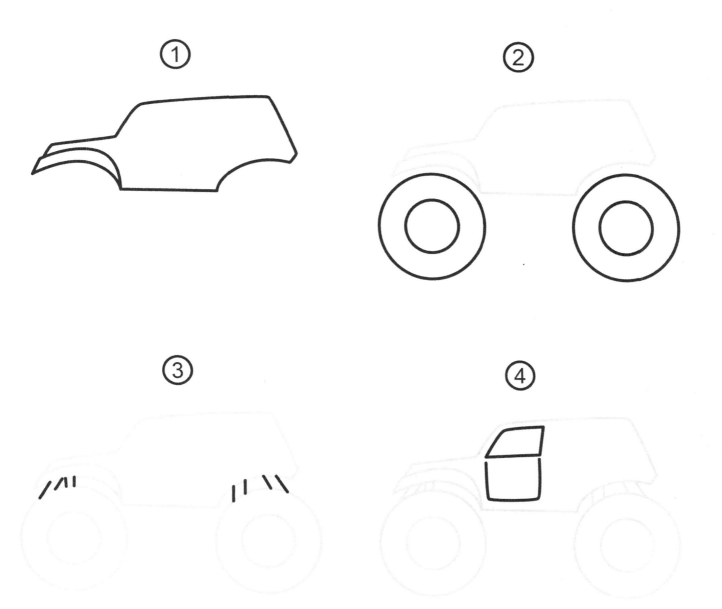

① ② ③ ④

Monster Truck

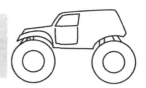

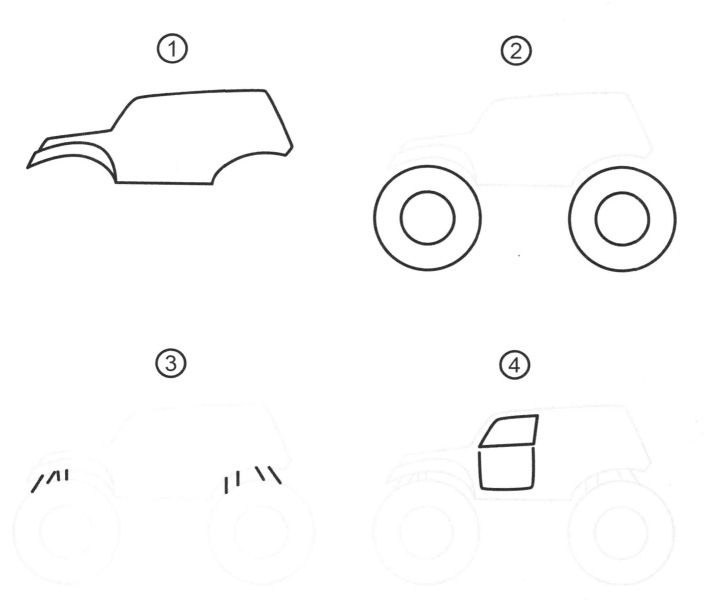

① ② ③ ④

①

②

③

④

Motorbike

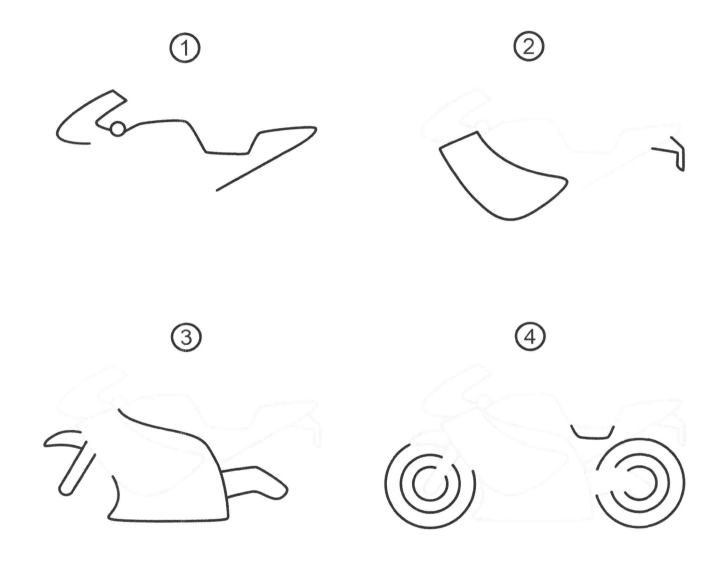

Speed Boat

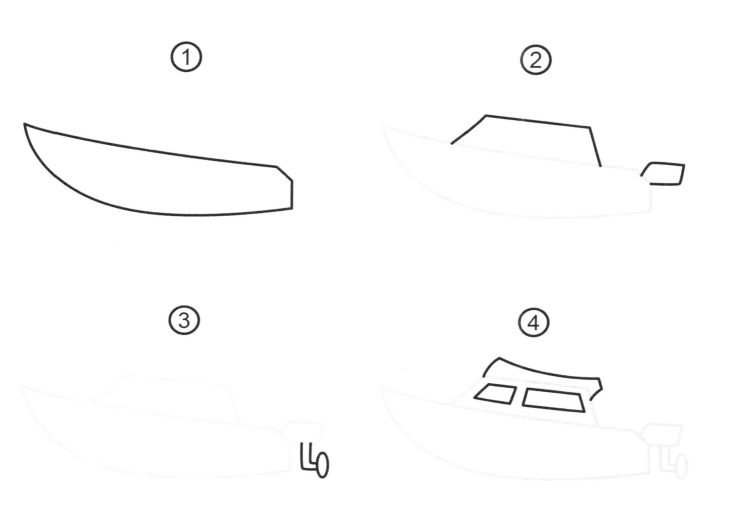

Sailing Boat

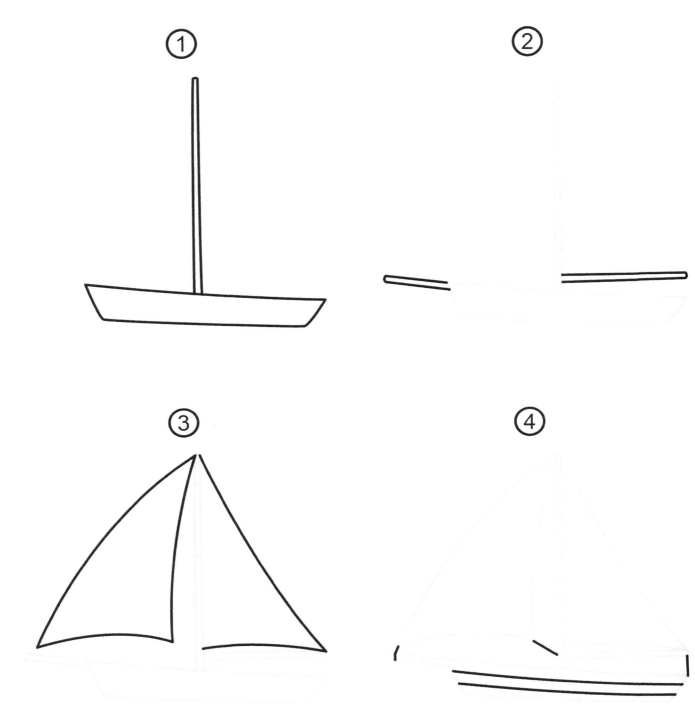

① ② ③ ④

Bicycle

①

②

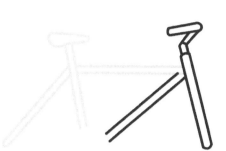

③

④

Train Steam Engine

① ②

③ ④

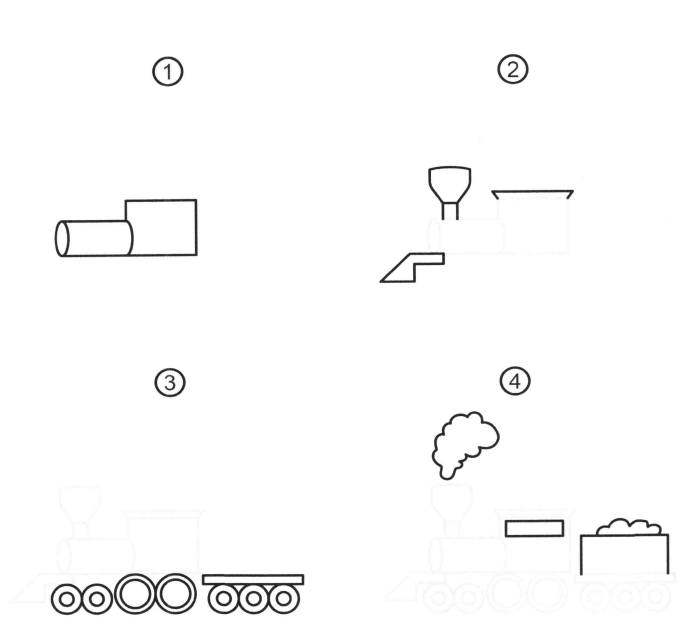

Fire Engine

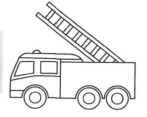

①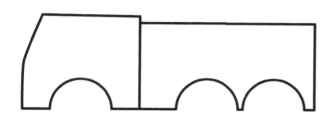

②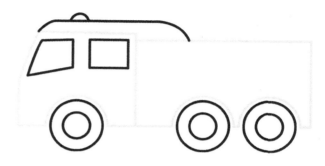

③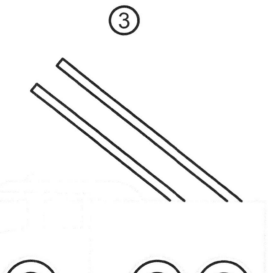

④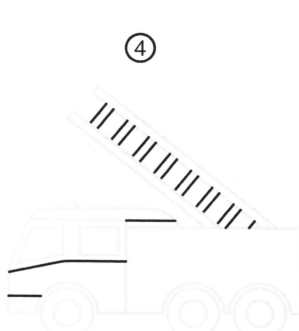

Police Car

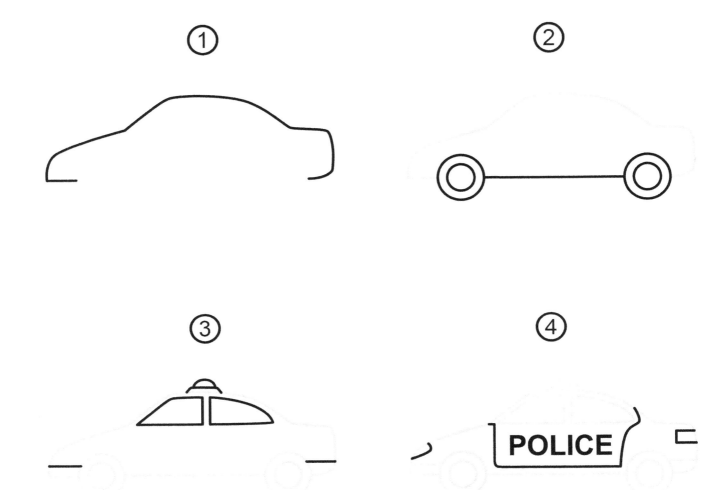

① ② ③ ④

Ambulance

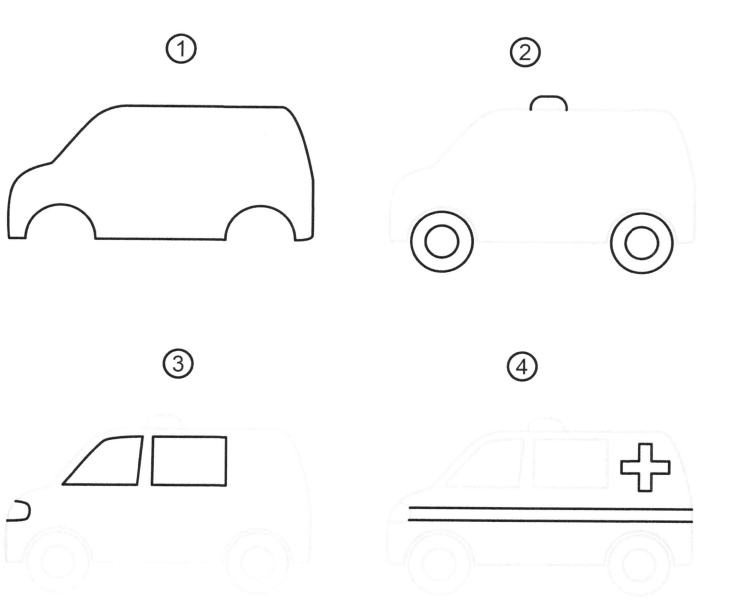

① ② ③ ④

Space Rocket

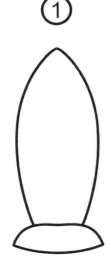

①

②

③

④

Vehicles and Machines

Helicopter

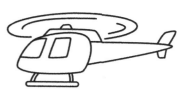

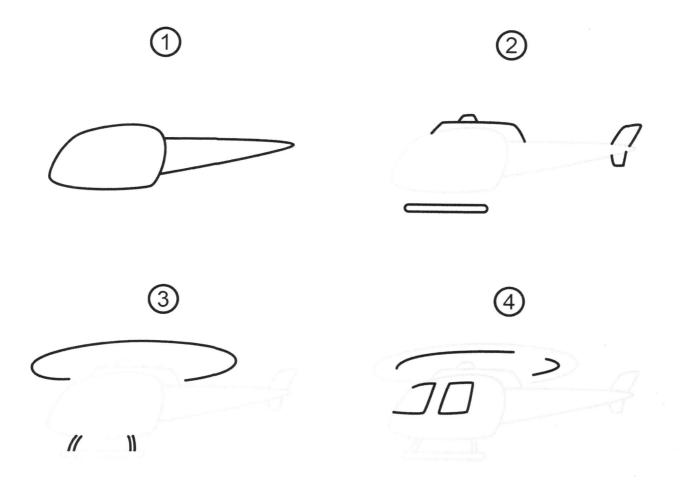

① ② ③ ④

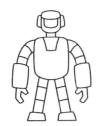

Robot

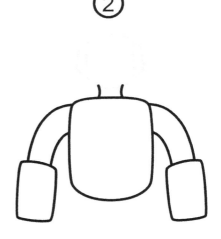

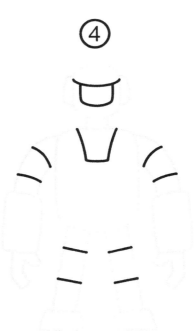

①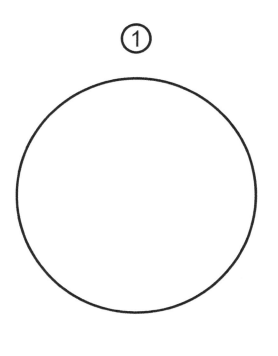

②

③

④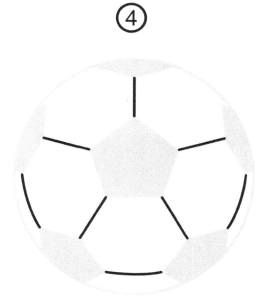

Apple

①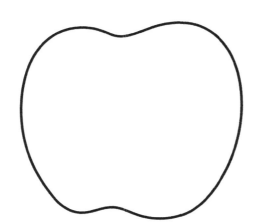

②

③

④

Rose

Sunflower

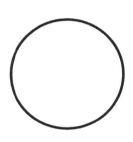

① ②

③ ④

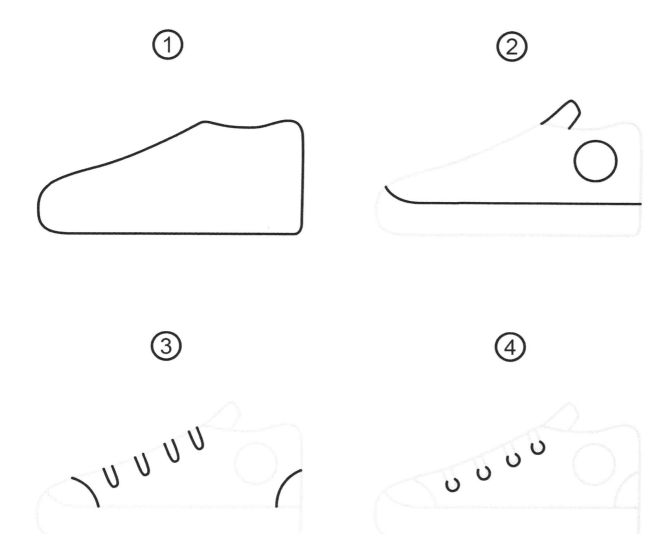

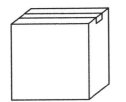

Box

①

②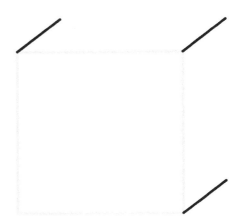

③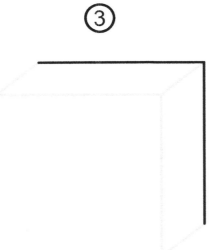

④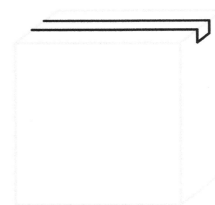

①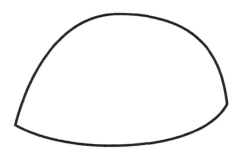

②

③

④

House

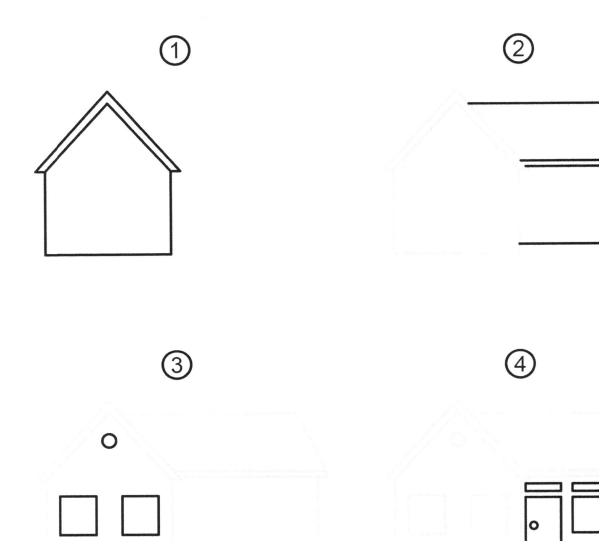

① ② ③ ④

Strawberry

Tree

①

②

③

④

①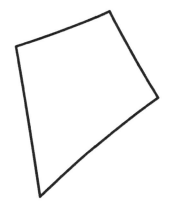

②

③

④

Guitar

①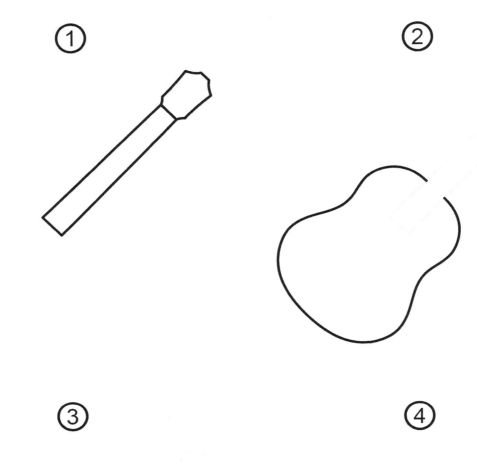

②

③ ④

Piano

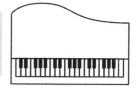

①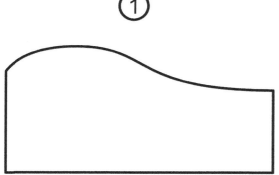

②

③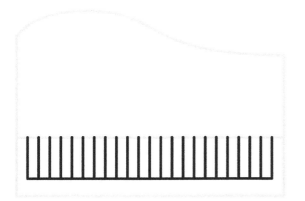

④

Tennis Racquet

①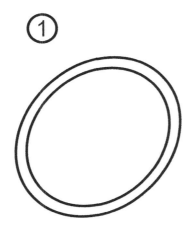

②

③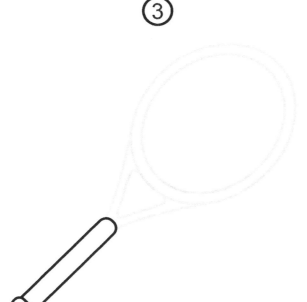

④

Rainbow

①

②

③

④

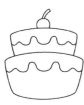

Cake

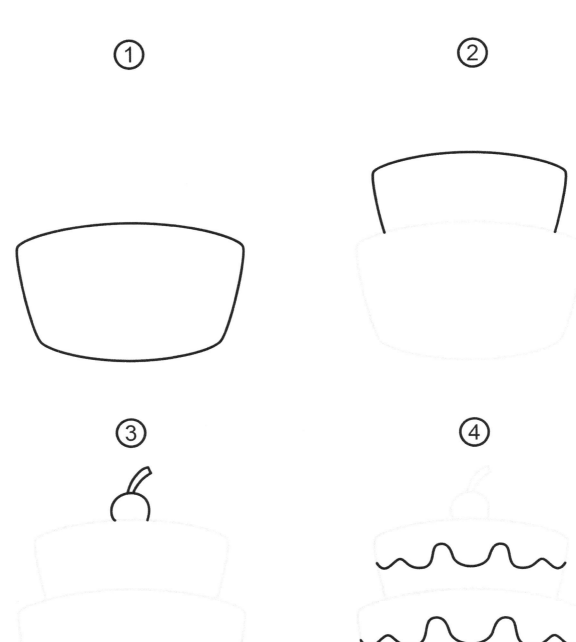

① ② ③ ④

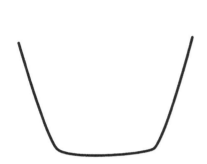

Cup

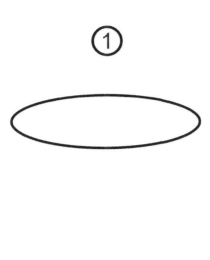 ①

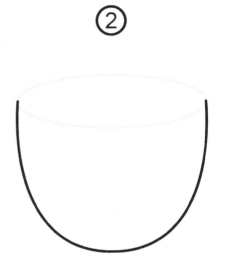 ②

 ③

 ④

Moon

① ② ③ ④

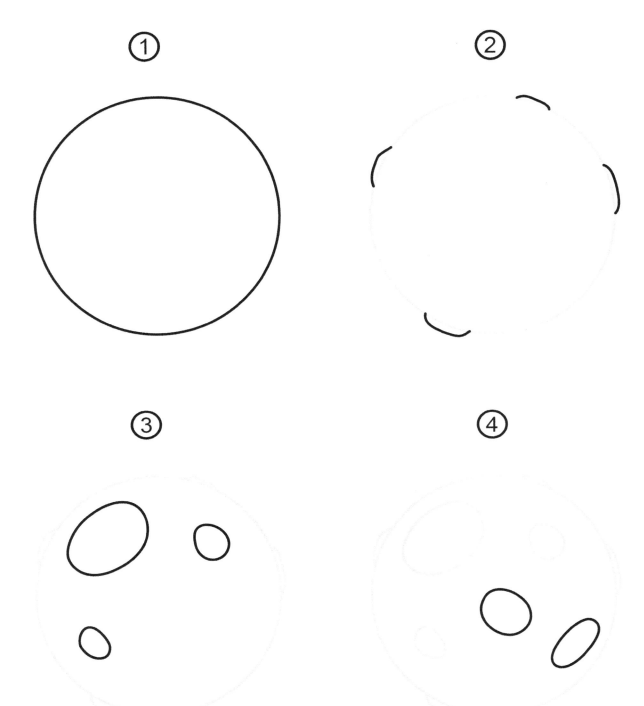

Umbrella

①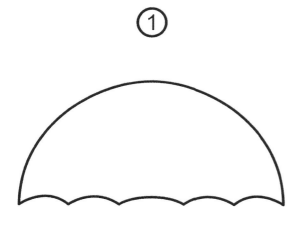

②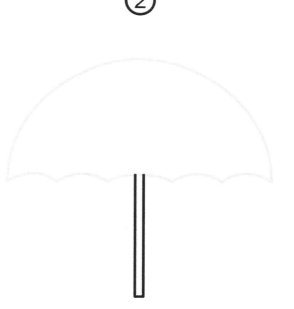

③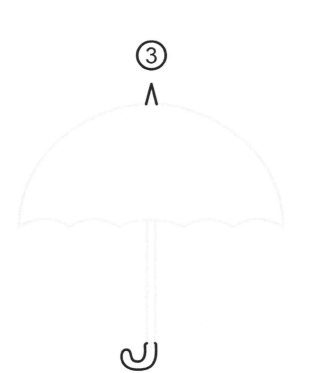

④

Woollen Hat

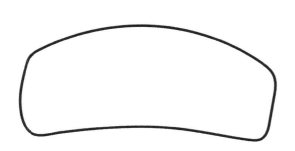

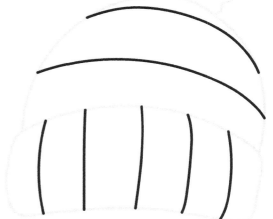

①

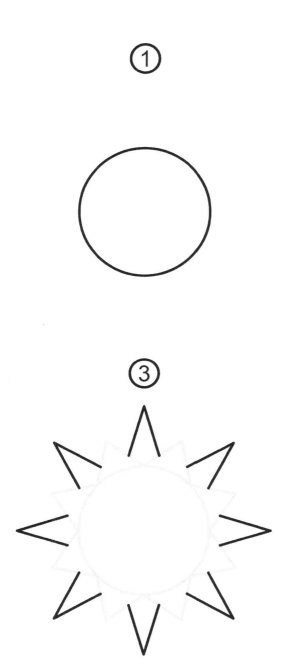

②

③

④

Pencil

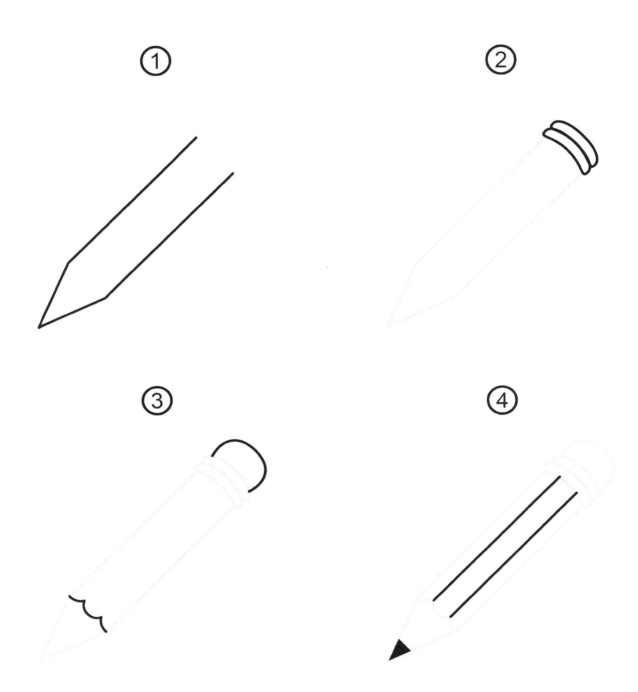

① ② ③ ④

Ice Cream Cone

①

②

③

④

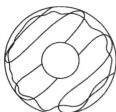

Donut

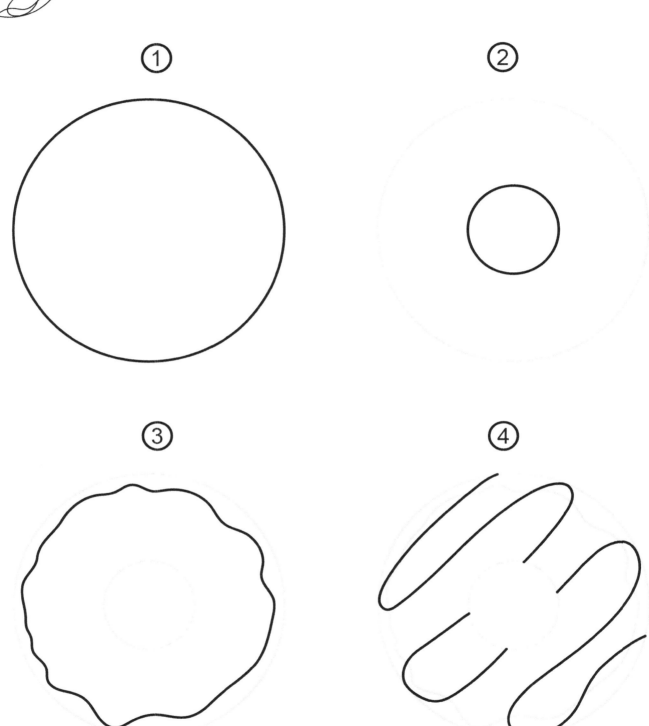

① ② ③ ④

①

②

③

④

Book

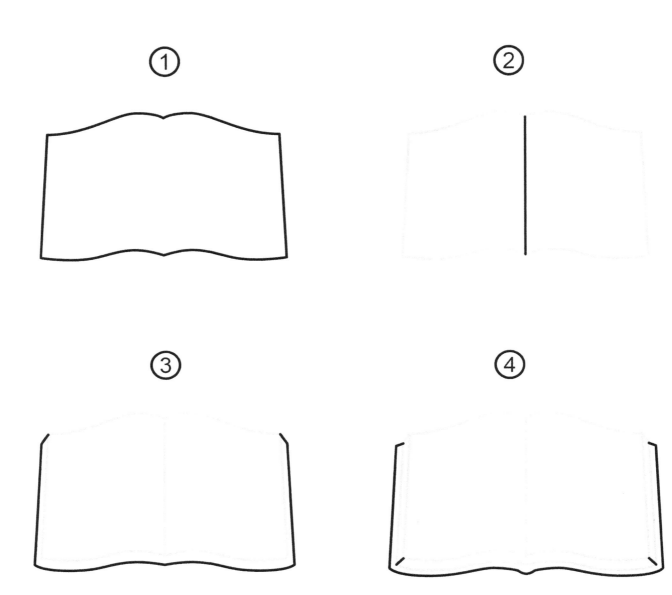

① ② ③ ④

①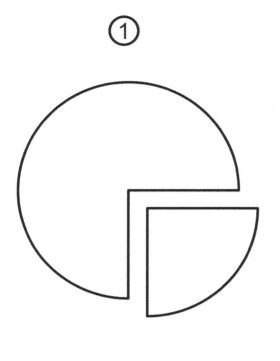

②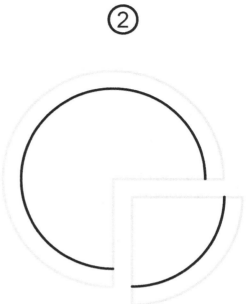

③

④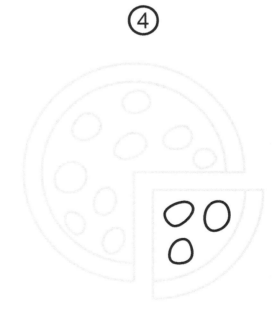

Saturn

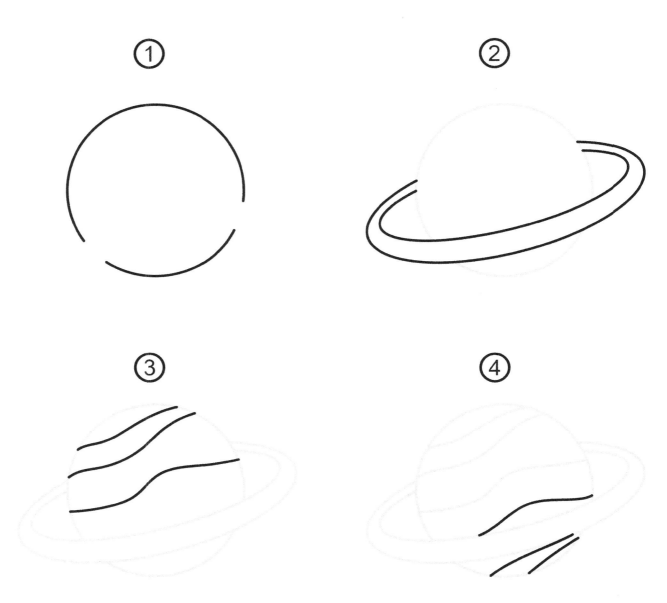

① ② ③ ④

①

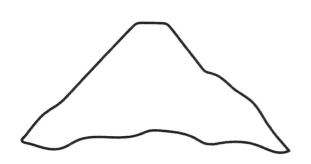

②

③

④

Backpack

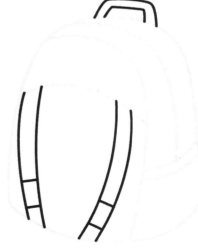

①

②

③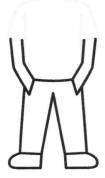

④

Woman

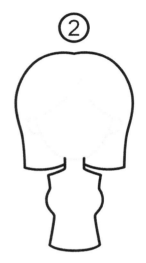

①

②

③

④

Hand

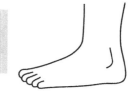

①

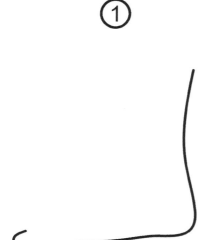

②

③

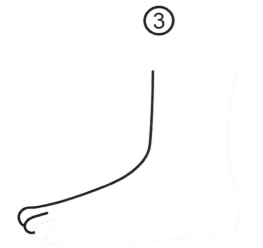

④

Smiling Face

①

②

③

④

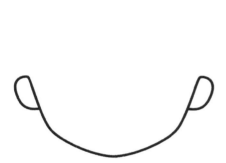

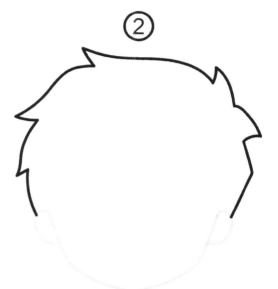

Angry Face

①

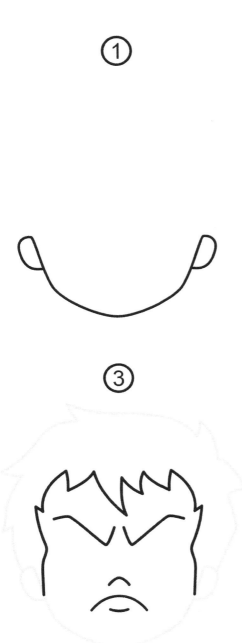

②

③

④

①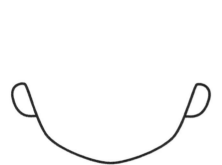

②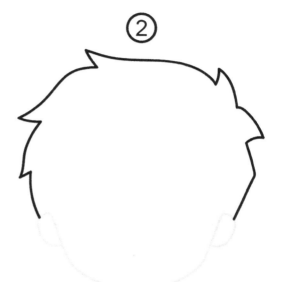

③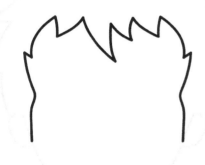

④

Person Running

①

②

③

④

Person Skipping Rope

①

②

③

④

Astronaut

①

②

③

④

I hope you enjoyed this book!

I love hearing from readers and parents. Join my email newsletter by scanning the QR code below.

Scan the code to get free activity sheets, a free picture book and early reader copies of my new books for free:

Adrian Laurent
Childrens Book Author

Made in the USA
Middletown, DE
29 July 2022